# JIM BONES
# TEXAS
## IMAGES OF THE LANDSCAPE

PHOTOGRAPHY BY JIM BONES

WESTCLIFFE PUBLISHERS, INC. ENGLEWOOD, COLORADO

# CREDITS

International Standard Book Number:
ISBN 0-942394-16-X
Library of Congress Catalogue Card Number:
86-050062
Copyright, Photographs and Text: Jim Bones, 1986
Designer: Gerald Miller Simpson/Denver
Typographer: Edward A. Nies
Printer: Dai Nippon Printing Company, Ltd.
Tokyo, Japan
Publisher: Westcliffe Publishers, Inc.
Post Office Box 1261
Englewood, Colorado 80150-1261

*First frontispiece: Morning surf on Matagorda Island, Calhoun County*

*Second frontispiece: Red clouds at dawn over brush country, Live Oak County*

*Third frontispiece: Dogwood and pines, Tyler County*

*Title page: Log cabin in grasses and golden waves, Travis County*

*Right: Indian blankets and bluebonnets, Llano County*

# PREFACE

*"A man might reject the myths, but he would have to know many facts about its natural life and have imagination as well as knowledge before entering into a country's heart. The history of any land begins with nature, and all histories must end with nature."*

— *J. Frank Dobie* —

Texas — the very word has attained mythological proportions and like most myths, the state itself is preposterously big. Measuring 860 miles north to south and 770 miles east to west, it is larger than many nations and some of its western counties are bigger than a few eastern states. In keeping with its mythological reputation, it rises from sea level to 8,750 feet, and encompasses more than 267,000 square miles of wildly varied but closely interrelated geology, topography, soil and climate.

Scholars of such things divide Texas into four to ten distinct physiographic provinces, based primarily on the underlying geology and the plant and animal communities the land supports. I have chosen to present these images in seven regional groups. Beginning with the lowest in elevation and climbing to the highest, they are: the Gulf Coast, Rio Grande Plains, Eastern Forests and Prairie Savannas, Hill Country, Central Mineral Region, High Plains and Red Rolling Prairies, and the Western Mountains and Desert Basins.

Texas is often called the natural crossroads of the continent, with a greater diversity of native life forms than any other state. Lying at the south end of the Great Plains, Texas hosts plants and animals that stretch from the Gulf of Mexico into Canada. Rocky Mountain aspens and ponderosa pines descend into West Texas. The Southern deciduous forests end their migration in the Big Thicket piney woods and post oak savannas of East Texas. The dry Chihuahuan Desert reaches into the Big Bend region and the Lower Rio Grande Valley marks the northern extreme of tropical Mexican vegetation. Scattered elements of all these meet in Central Texas, where cypress trees may rise out of moist canyons to spread fine leaves beside prickly pear cactus, bluestem grass, junipers, red sage and yellow waves of coreopsis flowers.

The varied Texas climate is key to the distribution of its native inhabitants. Average temperatures decrease rapidly from Brownsville in the southern Rio Grande Valley, with an annual mean of 74°F, to Dalhart in the northern Panhandle, with an annual mean of only 54°F. Snow often blankets the High Plains and Western Mountains, but rarely whitens the south, central and eastern regions. The coldest temperature yet recorded was minus 23°F in the northern Panhandle, while the hottest was 129°F in the western Big Bend desert. Wide daily variations occur and in the spring and fall, as Canadian blue northers push south toward the tropics, the mercury can plummet more than 50°F in just an hour.

Overall, precipitation is probably the most influential natural factor affecting the diversity of Texas. Rainfall decreases rather uniformly east to west, from nearly five feet annually at Beaumont on the Louisiana border, to about half a foot at El Paso on the New Mexico state line. Rains are often erratic, however, and usually develop from moisture released by thunderstorms that accompany swift moving Pacific disturbances, Arctic cold fronts and tropical hurricanes spinning inland from the Gulf of Mexico.

Each year, cloud-borne moisture, equal to about 200 inches of rainfall, flows north across Texas from the sea. Ironically, the state is largely arid or semiarid and successive years of near drought, interrupted by occasional seasons of intense precipitation, conspire to make rainfall below average. May is often the wettest month. Midsummer is usually dry, but again in September and October cool showers bring on a second "spring" of wildflowers blooming golden-eyed into fall. The Western Mountains have a late summer rainy season with thundershowers typical of the desert southwest and the relatively uniform East Texas rains increase as warm fronts are drawn north in the wake of cold winter storms.

As might be expected in a state of such extremes, both drought and flood are common, and in any year, hail or violent tornadoes may instantly transpose a strip of dense forest or field of bright wildflowers into a barren landscape. But to the incidental enjoyment of Texans and visitors alike, Texas plants and animals have evolved in close harmony with the lightning, wind and rain.

The earliest rocks exposed at the heart of Texas are more than three billion years old. They are the eroded roots of mountains that were raised from the oceans and then weathered away long before any creatures moved upon the land. During the intervening period, what is now Texas has endured the repeated rise and fall of peaks and the cyclic advance and retreat of seas. As the great pageant of earthly life unfolded, many of its major characters left their stories in the stone pages of the Texas geologic record, but until the last 40,000 years or so there were no humans to see or read it.

The first Texans came from Asia by way of a northern land bridge at the close of the last Ice Age, drifting with huge herds of splendid animals that shifted their grazing in response to changes in climate, seasons and vegetation. These prehistoric peoples carried seeds and extended their range, yet never exceeded the ability of the land to reproduce. Hunting and gathering as they went, some of them stayed on while others eventually walked to the tip of South America. There were only about 10 million humans in the world at that time. Now there are nearly twice that many in Texas alone. The first Europeans to see this land sailed into the mouth of the Rio Grande from Spain in 1519. Explorers and missionaries followed soon after to chart this "Terra Incognita" and tame the original "savage" Texans. By 1681 the earliest permanent settlement was founded near what is now El Paso. The face of Texas had changed very little for thousands of years until the appearance of those early Europeans, but they brought with them saws, plows and herds of domestic livestock, the agents of accelerating change that in less than 300 years were to remake the image of the land forever. Just before 1700, the first cattle

*Broken sandstone and plains grasses, Randall County*

and sheep came north of the Rio Grande. Today Texas produces more beef cattle and sheep than any other state and is the center of the angora goat industry.

When Texas came into the Union nearly a century and a half ago, it was the largest prairie state and still on the "frontier." As the land was steadily used up, people simply moved on to greener pastures and repeated the familiar process that left much of the Old World a worn-out disaster. With the advent of the industrial revolution, in the late 1800's and the attendant invention of barbed wire, windmills and railroads, the rate of change shifted into high gear. It suddenly became possible and highly profitable to carve up the remaining wild heart of Texas and ship it off to distant markets. Few people cared or seemed aware that the rich grasslands went north and east in the bellies of cattle on those legendary drives out of Texas or that the primeval forests were swiftly stripped as if by a plague of giant locusts. Fewer still realized the true natural wealth of the soil and its ancient ability to reproduce were forever plundered.

Soaring food prices and the need for lumber during World War I delivered the final blow when ranchers, farmers and lumbermen stepped up production as their patriotic duty. The land was pushed to the breaking point, and inevitably gave out. Beat down and trampled, cleared and plowed, the organic treasure of the soil was finally exhausted. When the dry winds of the dust bowl era rolled in, there was precious little vegetation left to hold the soil in place and the best part of Texas blew away or washed into the sea. This is the shameful legacy we inherit today. Have we learned any meaningful lesson from all this?

Texans in general are a self-sufficient and boastful people, fiercely proud of their mythical homeland and this year they celebrate the 150th anniversary of Texas' national independence. A great deal of attention is being paid to the accumulated heritage of this brief moment in the overall history of the state, but very little appreciation is ever given to the sustaining source of that heritage — the multibillion-year-old natural land itself. It was wilderness with its native plants and animals that shaped the character of the first Texans even as they remade it in their newfound image, and it still shapes the destiny of today's inhabitants.

Tragically, little or no true wilderness remains in Texas, or anywhere else in the world for that matter. In our curious way we have been nearly everywhere, bending the land and its creatures to blind selfish desires. But places still exist where many of the native plants and animals continue to adapt to the everchanging world around us. These small islands of wildness contain the last centers of biological diversity that once made the great state of Texas so appealing to the first settlers.

Unfortunately, Texas has one of the smallest per capita systems of parkland in the United States, but it would not require any huge sacrifice to guarantee the preservation of its remaining native species. A network of sanctuaries set aside for the benefit of the wild survivors could provide an invaluable natural base with which to gauge the rate of change occurring in the environment and ensure the perpetuation of Texas' most valuable heritage. All that is needed is a change of heart which comes with understanding we are not separate from the plants and animals which sustain us. We all share the same helical strands of life and when a part dies, in a very real way, so do we.

The innate vitality of wild land is tremendous. All we must do is leave it alone and stop abusing, harassing and developing it into extinction. Just let it be and it will mend itself. That is what life does best. The living soil, the grasses, herbs, woody shrubs, forests and all the wonderful animals will come back, in ways different of course from anything we see now, but still beautiful and strong. If allowed to, the good Texas earth will go on adjusting perfectly well for billions of years. Not only can the wild places provide the future seed resources of our physical well-being, but also the eternal healing of our souls.

The word Texas is derived from an old Caddo Indian greeting, "Tayshas," meaning allies or friends. That is exactly what the land needs most right now, allies and friends sympathetic to the ways that made it what it was before we came. Here is a look at some of the loveliest native places that are left to us, with an eye toward showing how it might be restored if Texans so choose.

*Jim Bones*

# GULF COAST PRAIRIES & MARSHES

This warm, humid region of nearly level sandy plains has many slow moving rivers, creeks, bayous and marshes that drain into brackish coastal waters. It is primarily grassland with scattered woody motts of post oak, live oak and acacia. Prickly pear cactus is plentiful along with yucca, mangrove, saltbush and tamarisk. Freshwater ponds support water lilies, duckweed and arrowheads, while the margins of tidal bays, lagoons and estuaries are filled with saltwort, sedges and cordgrass. Just off the mainland shore, a series of barrier islands with wide sandy, shell-covered beaches and tall shifting dunes rise like pale ghosts from the waves. Here croton, purslane, railroad vines, sea oats and other salt-resistant grasses and sedges form living anchors against the constant wind.

Area: 9,500,000 acres.
Elevation: Sea level to 150 feet.
Annual rainfall: 30 inches to 50 inches.

*Sunrise from Padre Island, Kleberg County*

*Beach morning glories, Kleberg County*
*Sand waves on Padre Island, Kleberg County*

*Crab claw and shells, Kleberg County*
*Drift log and surf, Nueces County*

*Bluestem grass and daisies by sand dunes, Mustang Island, Nueces County*

*Beach primrose and sea oats on Padre Island dunes, Kleberg County*

*Overleaf: Sunrise at Boca Chica, Padre Island in the Gulf of Mexico, Cameron County*

*Saltwort on tidal flats, Aransas County*
*Sand dunes invading salt marsh, Nueces County*

*Coral sea purslane and wind-blown grasses, Padre Island, Kleberg County*

*Salt flats by Copano Bay, Aransas County*

*Cord grass and railroad vines, Kleberg County*

*Coquina shells on Padre Island, Kenedy County*

*Overleaf: Dawn light on Matagorda Island,*
*Calhoun County*

*Oyster shells, portulaca, bayberries and oak leaves,*
*Aransas County*

*Salt marsh, Aransas County*

*Overleaf: Freshwater marsh and oak mott,*
*Aransas County*

# RIO GRANDE PLAINS

In this region level to rolling countryside is dissected by numerous arroyos and small streams that flow into the Rio Grande. The climate is hot and humid despite the relatively low precipitation. Vegetation is a mixture of open prairie on the uplands, with areas of dense thorny brush such as cacti, yucca, ebony, granjeno, guayacan, catclaw, black brush, white brush, wild olive, cenizo and mesquite. Willows and cottonwoods line the waterways. In the extreme lower portion of the near tropical Rio Grande Delta, a few small groves of the native Texas palm still survive.

Area: 20,000,000 acres.
Elevation: 10 feet to 1,000 feet.
Annual rainfall: 16 inches to 30 inches.

*Native Rio Grande Valley palm, Cameron County*

*Overleaf: Acacia, sage and ebony covered brush country, Valverde County*

*Ancient mesquite bark, Starr County*
*Thorn brush and sage, Zapata County*

*Willows and grassy islands in the Rio Grande,*
*Starr County*

*Willow leaves on still water, Starr County*

*Spanish moss in river woodlands, Hidalgo County*
*Wild olive, grass and mesquite, Starr County*

# EASTERN FORESTS & PRAIRIES

The topography of this extremely moist, complex region of interrelated provinces varies from flat plains to broadly rolling hills. Many wide, deep rivers and streams drain an area that changes dramatically from dense cypress swamps, palmetto bogs, beech, bay, magnolia, maple and hickory forests in the southeast to wide flower-covered prairies and oak wood savannas in the northwest. Where pines dominate, open parklands persist. The wetter parts are filled with an incredibly diverse assortment of orchids, carniverous plants, mosses, fungi, ferns, flowering shrubs and rare shade-loving species.

Area: Piney woods and deciduous forests –
   15,000,000 acres.
   Post Oak Savanna – 8,500,000 acres.
   Blackland Prairies – 11,500,000 acres.
   Cross Timbers and Prairies – 17,000,000 acres.
Elevation: 10 feet to 800 feet.
Annual rainfall: 35 inches to 60 inches.

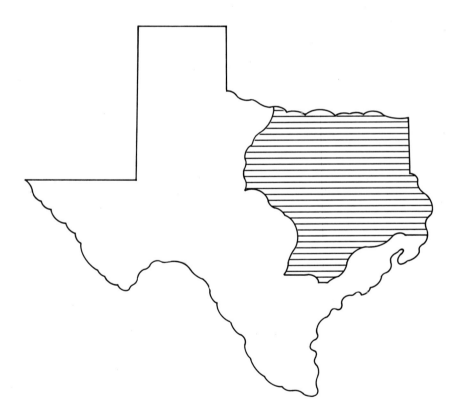

*Water lilies and hyacinths in a shallow pond,*
*Tyler County*

*Cone flowers and sensitive briar, Hardin County*
*Woodville pine forest, Tyler County*

*Bog moss, Hardin County*
*Dawn mist on a grassy lake, Hardin County*

Swamp honeysuckle, Tyler County

Yellow primrose, winecups and prairie bluebonnets,
Fayette County

Overleaf: Cypress knees and trunks by the Neches
River, Jasper County

*Swamp grass and mossy cypress knees, Tyler County*
*Beech and cypress by Wolfe Creek, Tyler County*

*Polypody ferns on a beech trunk, Tyler County*
*Fungi on beech roots, Tyler County*

Bog orchid, pitcher plants and ferns, Hardin County

Prairie bluebonnets and Indian paintbrush,
Austin County

Overleaf: Indian paintbrush, lamb's quarters and blue-
eyed grass, Gonzales County

*Red phlox and Indian paintbrush, Gonzales County*
*Pink primroses and grass, Gonzales County*

*Balloon vine pods, Gonzales County*
*Moss and lichens on a magnolia trunk, Hardin County*

*Maple, oak and fern leaves, Hardin County*
*Beech and magnolia trees, Hardin County*
*Overleaf: Palmetto swamp, Gonzales County*

*Cypress swamp in autumn, Jasper County*
*Pond weed and fallen leaves, Tyler County*

*Boulder lichens and pine needles, Bastrop County*

*Pine needles, oak leaves and mushrooms,*
*Bastrop County*

*Red mushrooms growing through beech and magnolia
leaves, Hardin County*

*Pine cone, maple and oak leaves, Liberty County*

*Overleaf: Autumn sunrise through cypress trees,
Jasper County*

*Spanish moss and cypress leaves, Harrison County*
*Cypress trunks by Caddo Lake, Harrison County*
*Overleaf: Winter brush and red grass, Wise County*

*Snake skin and leaves by the Trinity River,*
*Denton County*

*Cypress trees in Caddo Lake, Harrison County*

# HILL COUNTRY

The Hill Country is a highly dissected plateau with deep river canyons, clear spring-fed streams and rounded limestone ridges. The area is predominately grassy cactus-studded rangeland interspersed with yucca, Spanish oak, live oak, ash, elm, juniper and mesquite. The river bottoms also support magnificent stands of cypress and sycamore trees. These are often bent and twisted by the frequent floods that roar through narrow, cliff-walled valleys. In contrast, the upland surface tends to be dry, rough and rocky, indicating the transitional nature of this semiarid region.

Area: 22,000,000 acres.
Elevation: 800 feet to 3,000 feet.
Annual rainfall: 15 inches to 35 inches.

*Sunrise on frosty trees and grasses, Blanco County*

*Wet rocks and rain-soaked grasses, Blanco County*
*Morning dew on golden grasses, Travis County*

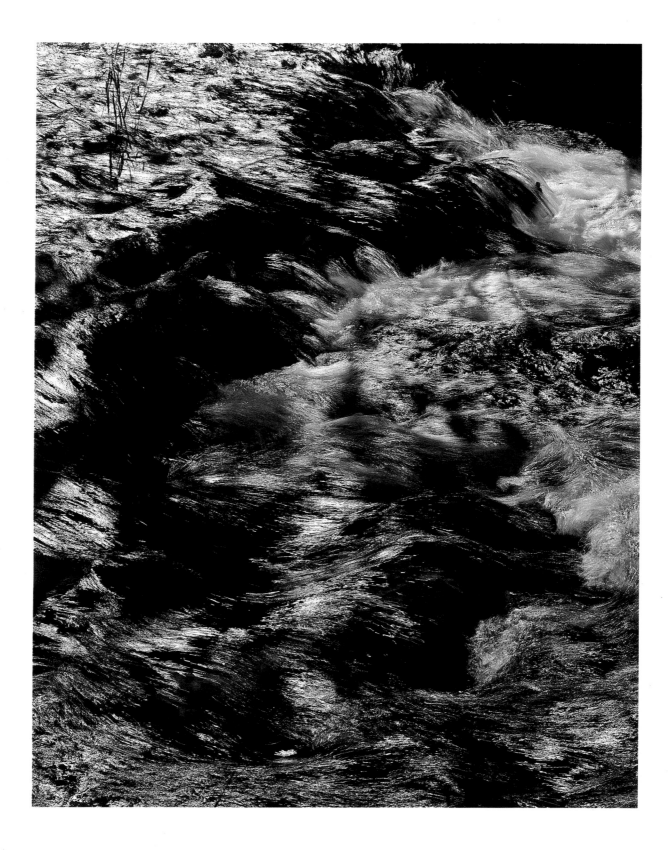

*Clear water in Barton Creek, Travis County*
*Frost on flood-twisted juniper, Travis County*

*Autumn rain on cactus, grass, and tree-covered hills,
Travis County*

*Indian grass and sycamore by Bull Creek,
Travis County*

*Overleaf: Mist over the Colorado River, Travis County*

*Wet juniper roots and elm leaves, Hays County*

*Cypress, willow and sycamore trees by the Colorado River, Travis County*

*Rain-soaked leaves and grass heads, Hays County*
*Freezing rain on grasses and live oak log, Travis County*

*Bent grasses glazed by an ice storm, Travis County*
*Yucca and live oak after an ice storm, Travis County*
*Overleaf: Roll clouds at the front of a blue norther,*
*Blanco County*

*Icicles and snow on a frozen spring, Hays County*

*Ice-bound branches below dripping springs,*
*Hays County*

*Frozen mushrooms and grass in late winter snow,*
*Blanco County*

*Freezing fog on redbud, juniper and grasses,*
*Blanco County*

*Ferns and cedar sage by seeping springs,*
*Uvalde County*

*Spring leaves on creek elms, hackberries and*
*sycamores, Travis County*

*Overleaf: Golden waves of coreopsis flowers,*
*Kendall County*

*Lace cactus blooming on broken limestone,*
*Hays County*

*Yellow prickly pear cactus and wild carrot flowers,*
*Kendall County*

*Cypress trees and flood piled stones, Real County*

*Button bush blooming by creek bottom rocks,*
*Travis County*

*Golden eyes and tumbled boulders by a deep creek hole, Travis County*

*Indian blanket, horsemint and thistles fill a summer field, Blanco County*

*Overleaf: Prickly pear cactus and brush surround a grassy clearing, Travis County*

*Wild morning glory blooming in a greenbriar thicket,*
*Travis County*

*Vines and trees by a wet weather creek, Travis County*

*Juniper and bluestem grass in summer colors,*
*Blanco County*

*Evening cirrus clouds ahead of a storm, Hays County*

# CENTRAL MINERAL REGION

A small, distinct section of rolling hills and deep river valleys lies at the very heart of Texas. The unique character of this semiarid land results from the eroded roots of what must have been splendid mountains, perhaps 12,000 feet high. First uplifted more than a billion years ago, the bedrock exposed here consists of pink granite domes surrounded by mineral-bearing metamorphic stones like gneiss and schist, some of which are over 3 billion years old. Grasses scattered with cacti and yucca dominate the landscape where soil is deep, with thickets of oak, juniper, mesquite and stream bottom groves of native pecan trees. In many places strange insulbergs or island rocks of bald granite rise smooth and shining, completely devoid of soil or vegetation.

Area: 2,000,000 acres.
Elevation: 1,000 feet to 2,000 feet.
Annual rainfall: 20 inches to 25 inches.

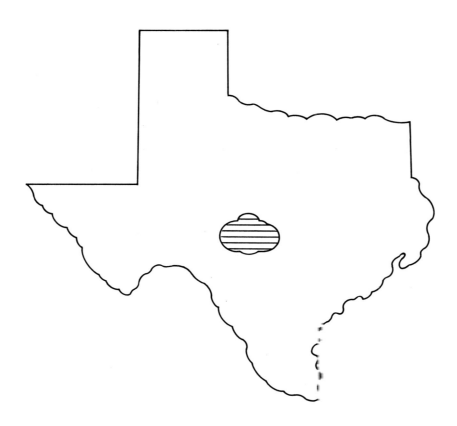

*Lichen galaxies on Precambrian granite, Burnet County*
*Overleaf: Clear Creek Falls tumbling over metamorphic rock, Burnet County*

*Granite outliers and parched grass, Llano County*

*Mineral-stained granite in a dry creek bed,*
*Llano County*

*Live oak leaves and catkins on lichen-covered granite,*
*Burnet County*

*Remnant ferns and old lichens, Burnet County*

*Metamorphic boulders and rain-spattered sand,*
*Llano County*

*Cactus, grass, yucca and nolina share soil in a stone*
*basin, Gillespie County*

*Overleaf: Oak forest ascending granite insulbergs and*
*Enchanted Rock, Gillespie County*

*Granite boulders weather from the roots of ancient mountains, Gillespie County*

*Algae in clear water on smooth stone, Burnet County*

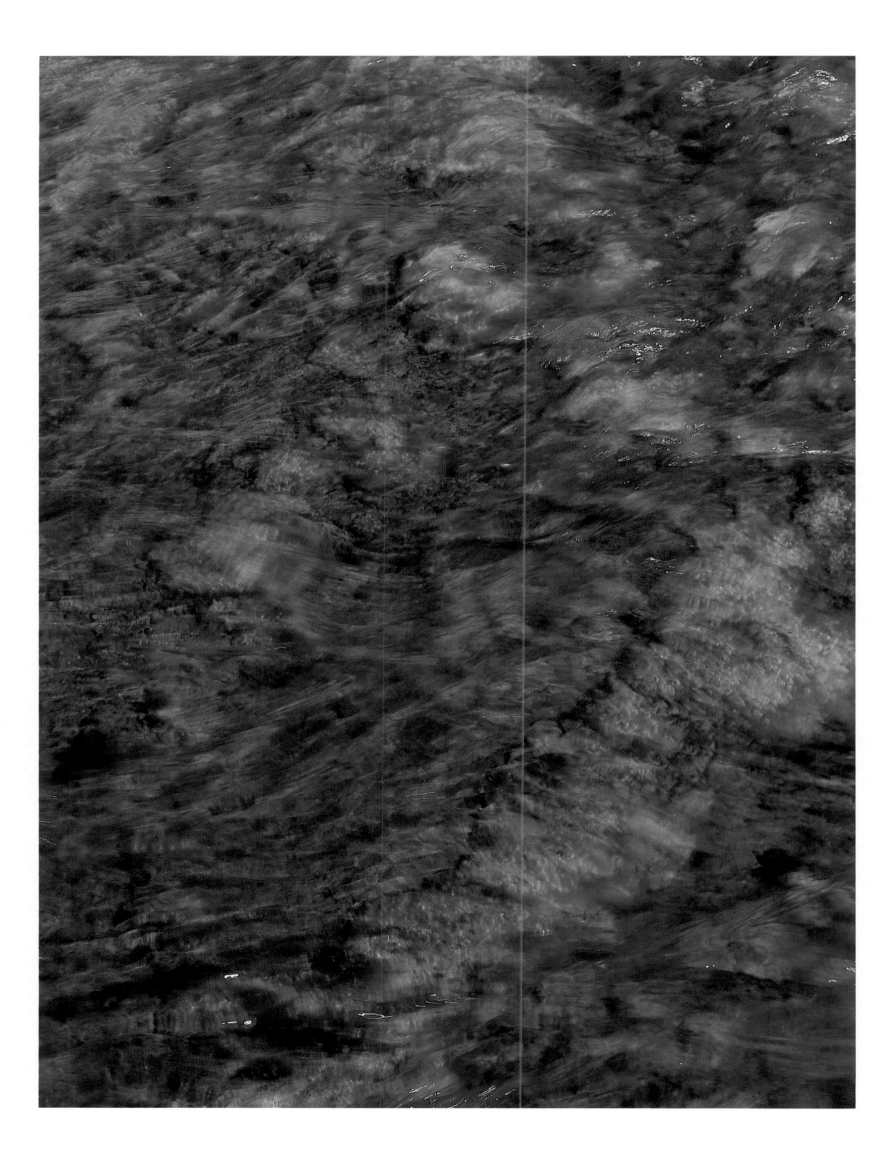

# HIGH PLAINS & RED ROLLING PRAIRIES

The Red Rolling Prairies on the east exhibit gentle to moderately rough topography, split by narrow, intermittent streams and a few wide sandy rivers. This area is distinctly separated by the Cap Rock Escarpment from the nearly level High Plains to the west. The surface of the incredibly flat, short grass-covered Llano Estacado, or Staked Plain, is dotted with numerous shallow basins called playas which hold water only after seasonal rains. The lower rolling portions sustain tall to mid-grass prairies with cactus, yucca and brushy invaders such as mesquite and juniper. Dwarf forests of shinnery oak and sand sage are also common. Cottonwoods, the only large trees native to the plains, are restricted to breaks along major streams. This high, dry region is hot in summer, cold in winter and the wind nearly always blows.

Area: High Plains – 20,000,000 acres.
        Red Rolling Prairies – 24,000,000 acres.
Elevation: 300 feet to 4,500 feet.
Annual rainfall: 15 inches to 30 inches.

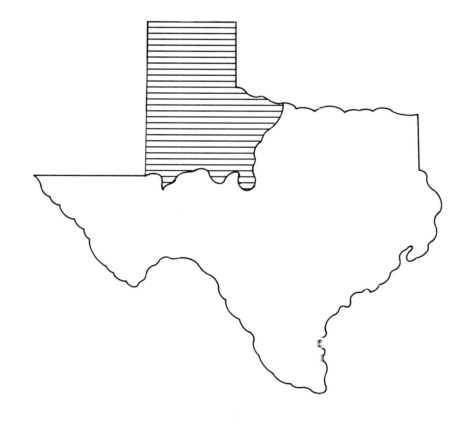

*Eroded fin at the edge of the High Plains,*
*Armstrong County*

Cottonwoods and canyon walls, Randall County

Layered sandstone and gypsum bacon rock,
Armstrong County

Overleaf: Juniper-covered breaks at the edge of the
Caprock, Randall County

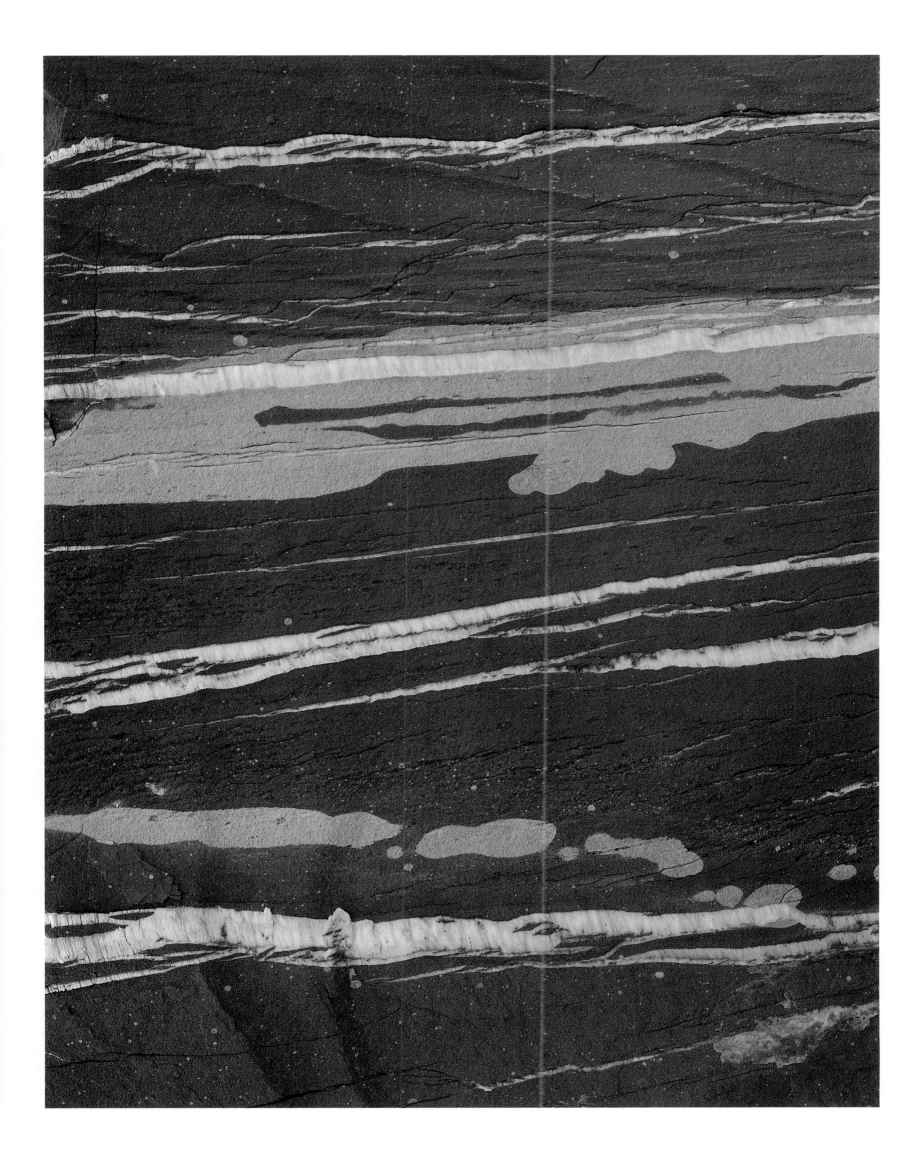

*Lightning on the plains west of Odessa, Ector County*

*Flood-rippled sand in Palo Duro Canyon,
Randall County*

*Tumbleweeds and concretions on red-rolling prairie,*
*Armstrong County*

*Flat plains grasslands, Deaf Smith County*

*Clouds spread over the red rolling prairie,*
*Fisher County*

*Reflections on the Prairie Dog Town Fork of the Red*
*River, Randall County*

*Overleaf: Red clay Spanish skirts erode in Palo Duro*
*Canyon, Randall County*

*Clay arroyo walls and mesquite scrub brush,*
*Armstrong County*

*Pink windmills bloom on adobe clay, Armstrong County*

*Sunflowers and tumbleweed on fallen sandstone cliffs,*
*Randall County*

*Grasses and junipers at the edge of the High Plains,*
*Randall County*

*Sage, goldenrod and dry grass, Randall County*

*Sunbleached Palo Duro Canyon juniper,*
*Armstrong County*

*Overleaf: Relict bigtooth maples, Culberson County*

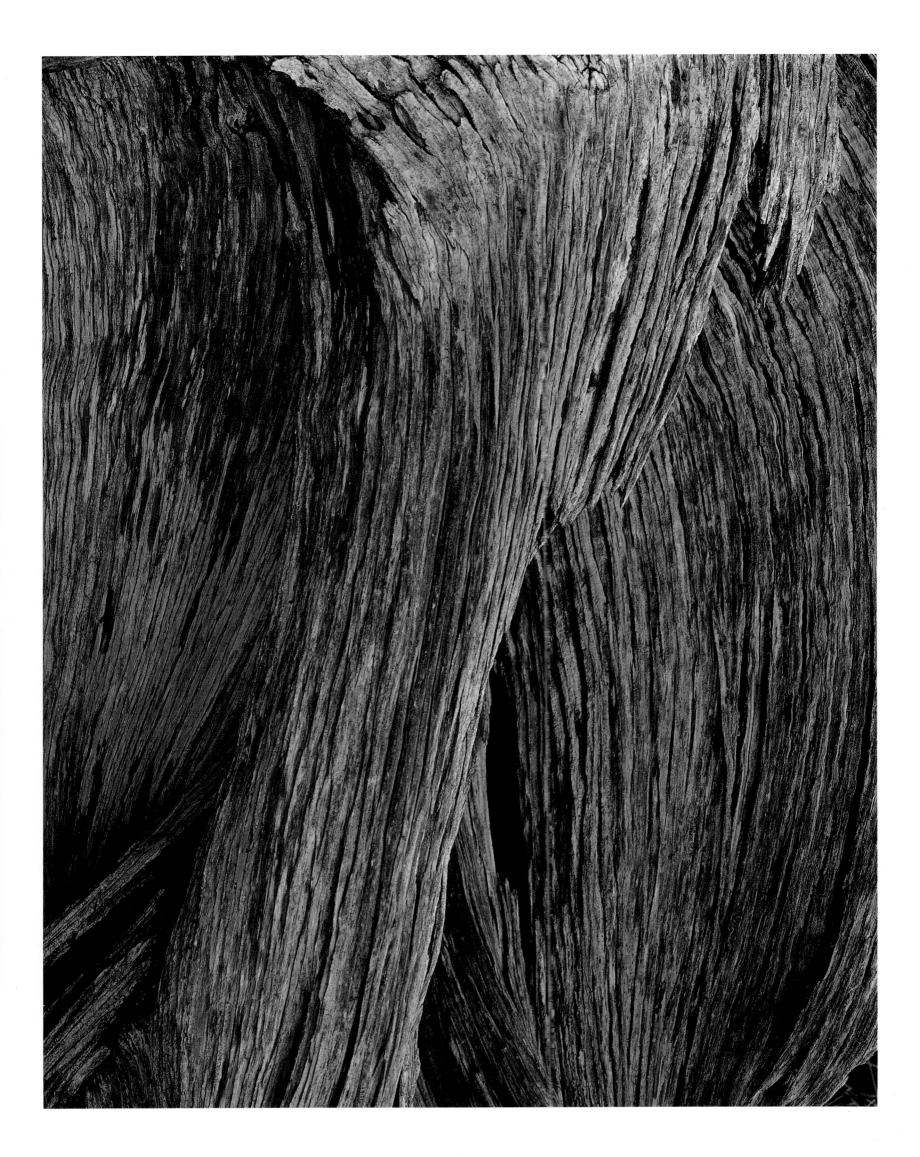

# WESTERN MOUNTAINS & DESERT BASINS

This region of both hot and cold extremes, consists of rugged highlands and arid valleys which display the most varied topography in Texas. The land rises from a deeply carved arid plateau along the Pecos River to join the Basin and Range Province at the southeastern end of the Rocky Mountains. Many ancient volcanoes stand shoulder to shoulder with uplifted fossil seabeds and the sandy shores of the geological past. Vegetation changes rapidly with altitude, from dusty salt basins nearly devoid of life, through shrubby Chihuahuan Desert grasslands, filled with lechuguilla, ocotillo, creosote bush, acacia, cacti, yucca, agave, sotol and mesquite. The upper elevations support moderate populations of tall grass, juniper, oak, madrone, pinyon and ponderosa pine. The highest, wettest peaks harbor relict stands of fir, aspen and maple left over from the Ice Ages of the Pleistocene.

Area: 19,000,000 acres.
Elevation: 2,000 feet to 8,750 feet.
Annual rainfall: 6 inches to 24 inches.

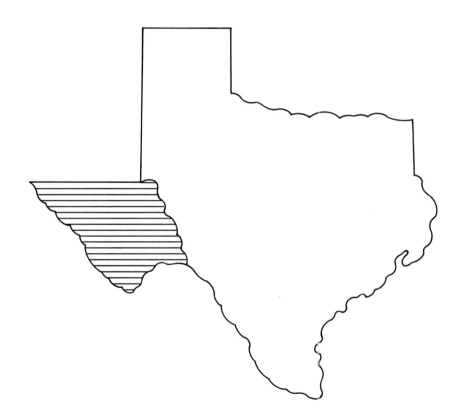

*Sandstone boulders below the Guadalupe Mountains,*
*Culberson County*

*Bunch grass on volcanic soil, Brewster County*

*Chihuahuan Desert agave succeed Chisos Mountain
oak, Brewster County*

*Cracked flood mud along a side arroyo,*
*Brewster County*

*Sunrise in Mariscal Canyon, near the Big Bend of the*
*Rio Grande, Brewster County*

*Overleaf: Snow on pinion pine and live oak in the*
*Davis Mountains, Jeff Davis County*

*Late sunflowers and early snow in the Guadalupe
Mountains, Culberson County*

*Snow-covered yuccas and brushy hills in the Guadalupe
Mountains, Culberson County*

Evening light on Maravillas Rapid in the Rio Grande,
Brewster County

Stormy sunrise over Black Gap, Brewster County

*Desert canyon waterfall, Presidio County*

*Golden baileya and yuccas blooming near the Eagle Mountains, Hudspeth County*

*Overleaf: Lava remnants on volcanic ash, Brewster County*

*Rock nettles on limestone cliffs, Brewster County*
*Algae and alkali in Tornillo Creek, Brewster County*

*Madrone tree with peeling bark, Jeff Davis County*

*Rain water cascading over volcanic rimrock,*
*Presidio County*

*Desert twilight south of the Chisos Mountains,*
*Brewster County*

*Cactus, lechuguilla, ocotillo and grasses on broken*
*ground, Brewster County*

*Overleaf: Morning mist in the Dead Horse Mountains,*
*Brewster County*

*Rio Grande sandbars and Pico del Carmen in Boquillas Canyon, Brewster County*

*Mexican buckeye flowering by seeps in a bedrock arroyo, Brewster County*

*Strawberry pitaya cactus, Brewster County*

*Morning clouds over Cerro del Barco and the Rio
Grande, Brewster County*

*Clouds on the Sierra del Carmen above Hot Springs
Canyon, Brewster County*

*Rio Grande-sculptured boulders in Santa Elena
Canyon, Brewster County*

*Overleaf: Ocotillo stalks in bloom, Brewster County*

*Reflections in Santa Elena Canyon, Brewster County*
*Desert below the South Rim of the Chisos Mountains,*
*Brewster County*

# TECHNICAL
# INFORMATION

The photographs within this book were made with a Toyo 4″ × 5″ field view camera, using lenses of 90mm, 120mm, 150mm, 180mm, 210mm and 300mm focal lengths.

Ektachrome daylight transparency film was used exclusively. Exposures were calculated with a Pentax Digital 1° spot meter and a Gossen Luna-Pro light meter. Both incident and reflected values were measured in conjunction with a gray card. Apertures range from f/11 to f/64. Exposures varied from 1/50 second to several minutes. Yellow, red and magenta gelatin filters were used to correct for the reciprocity failure of the film during long exposures and in cloudy or shaded conditions to adjust for the imbalances related to the dyes in the film.

The transparencies were separated on state-of-the-art laser scanning devices by the printer. Color reproduction was achieved with the goal of presenting the most beautiful interpretation possible of the original scene.